my first
CAT
BOOK

my first
CAT
BOOK

simple and fun ways to care
for your feline friend

for kids aged 7+

ANGELA HERLIHY

CICO **Kidz**

For Danny

Published in 2016 by CICO Kidz
An imprint of Ryland Peters & Small Ltd

20–21 Jockey's Fields   341 E 116th St
London WC1R 4BW   New York, NY 10029

www.rylandpeters.com

10 9 8 7 6 5 4 3 2 1

Text © Angela Herlihy 2016
Design, photography, and illustration
© CICO Books 2016

A CIP catalog record for this book is available from the Library of Congress and the British Library.

ISBN: 978 1 78249 380 8

Printed in China

Editor: Caroline West
Series consultant: Susan Akass
Designer: Barbara Zuñiga
Illustrator: Hannah George

In-house editor: Dawn Bates
In-house designer: Fahema Khanam
Art director: Sally Powell
Production manager: Gordana Simakovic
Publishing manager: Penny Craig
Publisher: Cindy Richards

Contents

Introduction

Hooray! You're getting a cat! That is wonderful news. You will find that owning a furry friend is a joyful experience and will bring you lots of fun.

Humans and cats have lived together for thousands of years, since the ancient Egyptians found they were good at catching mice, and we still value their company today. Cats are beautiful and fascinating creatures. They can be both independent and loving, amusing and relaxing to be around. When you want to play, they will race around with you but when you are tired or unwell, they will cuddle up next to you too.

Cats are the most popular pets in the world and you will soon see why. They can leap and race, climb and pounce, amaze you with their agility, and then spend the rest of the day asleep!

Owning any animal is a big responsibility. Remember that your cat is not a toy, but a living being who needs daily love and attention. In this book, you will find out how to be a kind and good owner. Chapter 1 will tell you where to get your cat or kitten from, and what you may need to buy. Chapter 2 explores your cat's behavior and habits, while you will learn how to care for and keep your cat healthy in Chapter 3. Best of all, the last chapter shows you how to make cat toys and which games your feline friend will love to play.

Most cats live for many years, so you will have a long friendship full of happiness and fun together. Whether you decide on a tiny, cute kitten or a wise, older cat, your life will never be the same again.

Enjoy your new furry best friend!

chapter 1

Preparing for your cat

Choosing your cat

Deciding to welcome a cat into your home is very exciting but, first of all, you should talk to your family about where the cat will come from. You'll also need to decide if you would like a kitten or cat, a pedigree cat or moggie, and whether you'd prefer a boy or girl.

Where to get your cat

There are many places that sell cats and you will need to decide which is best for you. These places might include:

- An advertisement in a store or newspaper, or on the Internet
- A local animal rehoming center or an animal welfare charity (see page 126)
- A cat breeder
- A friend whose cat has had kittens

It is important to visit the cat, especially if you are answering an advert or considering a cat you have seen on the Internet. If you are looking for a kitten, make sure the mother cat is with the kitten and that both are healthy. If you are getting your cat from a rehoming center or charity, they will want to talk to you and your family to ensure that they match you with the perfect pet. They may even want to visit you at home.

You'll also need to spend time playing with the cat to be sure you like each other—this is the fun bit! You will soon work out what kind of character your cat has—some cats are friendly and enjoy being picked up or stroked, while others are shy and nervous or even cheeky.

SAFETY FIRST

- Most rehoming centers and charities recommend against purchasing cats and kittens from pet stores because your new pet might find it difficult to socialize and be friendly, or she may even have health issues.

- It isn't advisable to provide a home for a stray cat. Strays are local cats who don't seem to have an owner. They may be friendly and want to come into your house. However, it's not usually a good idea to take in strays because you do not know anything about their background or behavior, or if they have any medical problems. They may even live in a house nearby!

- If you think it would be nice to give a stray cat a good home, contact your local rehoming center. They will have a large selection of cats that need homes and will know which cat is best for you.

Long-haired Persian cat

What type of cat?

We all have our favorite type of cat—silver tabby, black-and-white tuxedo cat, or maybe a long-haired breed. But did you know that there are two main cat groups: pedigrees and moggies?

Pedigrees: These cats are carefully bred by specialty breeders so that they have a reliable look or temperament. Examples of pedigrees include Siamese, Burmese, or Maine Coon cats. Some pedigrees have certain health problems or need particular care, such as daily grooming. Pedigrees can also be expensive to buy.

Moggies: These cats have a mixed heritage. Most of the cats you see are moggies. They are easy to come across and usually have fewer health issues than pedigrees. There are so many moggies around that they are often cheap to buy—or sometimes even free.

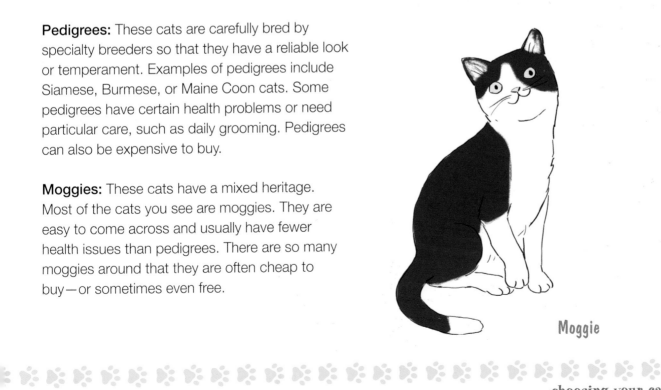

Moggie

Is the kitten ready to go?

If you have decided to get a kitten, you'll need to check that she is ready to leave her mother, which is usually at around 8–9 weeks old. By this time, a good home/rehoming center should have prepared her by ensuring that she is:

- **Socialized:** Your new kitten should be used to being handled by people.
- **Weaned:** She should be eating solid food rather than drinking her mother's milk.
- **Toilet-trained:** She should know how to go to the toilet in a litter tray (see pages 70–71).
- **Vaccinated:** Check that the vet has given her the first immunizations (injections) at 8–9 weeks old to keep her healthy (see page 73). Kittens need a second batch of injections when they are 12 weeks old.

Is she healthy?

A healthy cat or kitten will be sociable and alert. She should have clean, bright eyes, a soft coat, a clean bottom, and her nose should not be runny. She should breathe easily with no wheezing.

Boy or girl?

If you are choosing a kitten from a litter, you may need to decide whether to get a boy or a girl cat. Males tend to be more territorial than females and so often get into fights with neighboring cats, whereas females usually stay closer to home. You may find that a male cat acts more calmly if he is neutered. Neutering is a special operation performed by a vet to stop your cat breeding and having kittens (see page 74). There are lots of unwanted kittens born every year, so whether you get a boy or girl cat, neutering is recommended to prevent them breeding by accident.

Did you know?

Over 60 percent of ginger cats are male; all tortoiseshell cats are female; and most deaf cats are white-haired and blue-eyed. All of these traits are due to the cat's genetic make-up—the qualities they inherit from their parents.

Double trouble!

You might be tempted to take two kittens home with you. Two from the same litter is a better idea than two cats that do not know each other, as they will have formed a friendship already. However, two cats means two lots of food and bowls, two litter trays, two lots of vet's bills, and double the care and attention from their owners.

What to expect from your cat

There are so many choices to make when you want to get a cat. Should you have a new kitten or give a home to an older cat? What are the differences? The perfect cat is out there—you just need to think carefully about how she will fit into your life.

Kitten or cat?

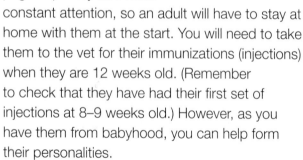

There's no doubt that a tiny, fluffy kitten is adorable, but perhaps an older cat might suit your family better.

Kittens: Little kittens are sweet, but hard work. They need feeding at least four times every day and may have to be reminded how to use a litter tray (see page 22). They also need constant attention, so an adult will have to stay at home with them at the start. You will need to take them to the vet for their immunizations (injections) when they are 12 weeks old. (Remember to check that they have had their first set of injections at 8–9 weeks old.) However, as you have them from babyhood, you can help form their personalities.

Cats: Older grown cats will already be house-trained and immunized. They have their own character, so you will need to choose one who is used to children and is happy to live with a family. Adult cats may also not be as playful and happy to be handled as a kitten at first. If you acquire an older cat from a rehoming center, the staff there will be able to tell you the cat's likes and dislikes.

! SAFETY FIRST

• Your new pet will be nervous when she first arrives, so be extra careful when handling her. She will feel overwhelmed by all the new smells, sights, and sounds in your house. If you try to pull her out of her hiding place, she may react by trying to scratch you, so give her time to come out when she is ready.

(For more advice on what to do when your cat first arrives home, see pages 32–35.)

Habits and handling

Because kittens are small, they are timid and easily injured. You need to hold them gently and speak quietly. Kittens are lively and jump about, so can easily get lost around the house (see page 28). Older cats might be shy to start with and take longer to be friendly but, with coaxing, they make lovely companions. (See Chapter 2 to learn more about picking up and handling your cat, as well as how to understand her behavior and body language.)

Indoor or outdoor?

Cats are independent animals that need lots of exercise. A safe home with outdoor space is ideal. There are some cats who, because of health reasons such as deafness or blindness, need to stay at home all the time. Indoor cats will need extra toys and play to ensure they keep fit and mentally active. Although they do not go out, a vet will still recommend immunizations in case they catch a disease from visitors.

If your cat is going to be allowed outside (see pages 80–83), you may want to think about putting a cat flap into your back door so that she can go out and come in when she wants to. You might need to teach your cat how to use the cat flap (see pages 85–86). However, you will need to keep her inside at first and it is always better to lock the cat flap and keep her indoors at night.

Your responsibilities

Cats are known for being much more independent and easier to look after than dogs, but our feline friends still need plenty of care and love. Your cat will depend on you and your family to meet her basic needs and she will reward you with lots of affection and companionship.

1 Commitment

When you give a cat a home, you are at the beginning of a long and happy friendship. This special relationship needs a commitment from you to look after your pet for her whole life and not to treat her as a toy that you can sometimes ignore.

2 Comfort

All pets need a suitable place to live and cats fit well into family life. Occasionally, your cat may become stressed by the noise of a busy home, so give her a safe place to hide away and sleep. A warm cushion or pillow or a cardboard box in a quiet room is cozy.

Feline fact

The average life span for a domestic cat is around 16–18 years, but the oldest cat ever was 38 years old. Her name was Creme Puff and she lived in Texas, USA.

3 Food and water

Cats need a fresh supply of food and water every day. Don't be tempted to feed your kitty food from your plate because lots of our food can be dangerous for cats (see page 29). Pet stores and grocery stores sell food that is specially designed for cats. Too many cat treats will lead to an overweight cat, so be aware of overfeeding her (see page 69).

4 Company

Although many people think of cats as solitary adventurers, most cats enjoy having a loving owner to come home to. A contented cat will relax when you stroke her and, when she is not sleepy, will play games with you and her toys.

Time away

As a responsible owner, you must be sure that your cat is going to be well looked after if your family is going away. A friend or neighbor can come in to feed your cat every day or you can book your pet into a local cattery. She will be delighted to see you when you come home!

5 Care when sick

Luckily, cats do not get ill very often but you should register your cat with a vet. The vet will know what to do if your cat isn't feeling well or is injured, and will also give her important immunizations to prevent illnesses. Take her to the vet for a health check annually when she has her vaccinations. This will help to spot any diseases early before they become serious.

Equipment your cat will need

Now you have chosen your cat, it's time to go shopping! It is tempting to buy all sorts of lovely things for your cat in pet stores, but you only actually need a few things to get started. Remember, if you are lucky enough to be welcoming two kittens, you will need two of everything!

1 **Cat carrier:** This is essential for transporting your cat home securely. It is not advisable to use a cardboard box, as your new pet may be frightened and claw her way out. A sturdy plastic box with a removable lid and a strong door flap is best. Do not buy a small one—your cat will grow quickly, and she will need room to sit up and lie down in her travel box on future visits to the vet.

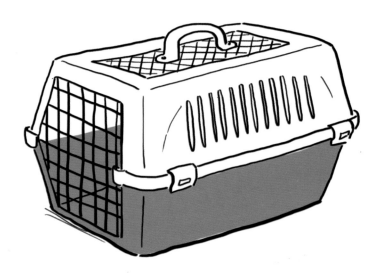

2 Food and water bowls: It is best to have separate bowls for food and water. These can be made of plastic, metal, or ceramic. A spare food bowl and water bowl can be useful because your cat's bowls will need washing regularly. Try to find small, shallow bowls for kittens. Cats will need bowls with non-slip bases.

3

Cat bed: Your new cat will need a bed so that she has somewhere warm and safe to sleep. She may also use it to hide in if she is feeling nervous. It can be as simple as a box or as fancy as a store-bought bed with a roof. (You can also make your own—see pages 24–27.)

Litter tray: While your cat becomes accustomed to her new home, she will be staying indoors. This means that she needs somewhere to go to the toilet! A litter tray is a large tray into which you pour cat litter. The tray must be washed regularly (in a suitable pet-friendly detergent), so it's best to choose a plastic one because this is the easiest to clean. You will also need a large sack of cat litter to go with it and a pair of latex (rubber) gloves for when you clean it out!

Scratching post: Cats have a natural instinct to scratch objects in order to sharpen their claws. Rather than letting your cat ruin the sofa, provide her with a scratching post. You can buy elaborate multi-level posts or make your cat a special scratching pad (see page 61).

6 **Collar:** Buy a "quick-release" or "safety" cat collar as this will snap apart if your cat gets it caught on a branch. Kittens will need to begin wearing a collar from around 3 or 4 months old, when they first go out into the garden. Remember to keep the collar loose—make sure you can fit two of your fingers between the collar and the cat's neck. You will also need to loosen it further as your kitten grows. Collars also come with bells and name tags attached.

7 **Toys:** Cats love to chase and pounce. You can buy very cheap cat toys in mice and fish shapes with bells and feathers, but it is also fun to make toys for your cat at home (see Chapter 4).

Make a cat bed

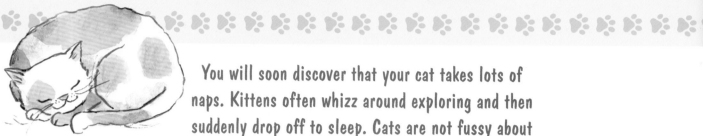

You will soon discover that your cat takes lots of naps. Kittens often whizz around exploring and then suddenly drop off to sleep. Cats are not fussy about where they sleep, but it is fun to make them their own special bed.

You will need

* A large cardboard box
* Scissors
* A pen or pencil
* A cushion or pillow
* A blanket or old sweater
* Newspapers

1 Find a cardboard box that is large enough for your cat to stretch out in.

2 Carefully cut off the top flaps with the scissors.

Cozy kitty

Have you noticed that your cat likes to sit in boxes, bags, or even the bathroom sink? The reason cats like being in confined spaces is because it makes them feel safe and secure. They also enjoy hiding where they can keep an eye on what is going on, while feeling nice and cozy.

3 Draw an opening on one side and cut it out. If this is tricky, ask an adult to help you.

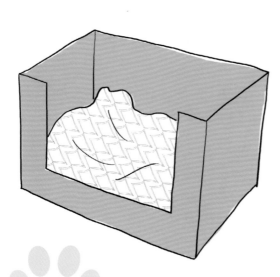

4 Lay a cushion or pillow in the base of the box, then put a blanket or old sweater on top.

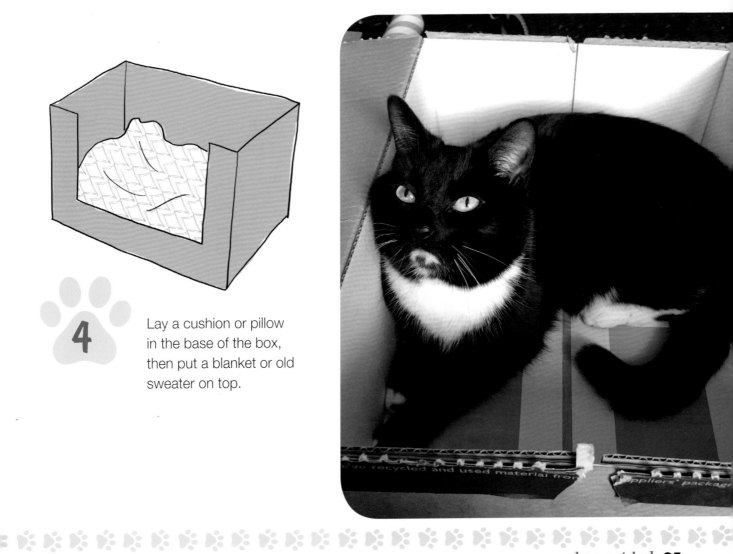

5

Put a few newspapers on the floor and then sit the bed on them. They will insulate the bed from the chilly floor.

6

Show your cat her lovely new bed. You may have to entice her in at first, but don't worry if she doesn't take to her new bed straightaway. If she is unsure, try placing the bed somewhere quiet and safe, rather than in the middle of a room.

It's fun to make your cat a SPECIAL bed

Feline fact

Cats can sleep for up to 16 hours per day. When your cat is sound asleep, her paws or whiskers might twitch, which shows she is having an exciting dream.

Keeping your cat safe

Cats and kittens are curious and like to investigate. Your cat will naturally want to explore her new house but you need to be aware of the dangers. She may get trapped somewhere or eat something poisonous, so it is sensible to make sure your family understands what could harm her.

Places to hide

Kittens trot around and poke their noses in small spaces. Try to keep your cat safe by:

- Ensuring that she doesn't get lost in the gaps between cupboards, up fireplaces, and in linen closets (airing cupboards)
- Keeping washing machine and tumble dryer doors closed
- Shutting cupboard doors
- Always keeping the lids on trash cans (rubbish bins) and putting toilet seats down

Also remember that cats and kittens may climb up drapes (curtains) and escape through open windows.

SAFETY FIRST

Most owners do not realize that many houseplants are poisonous to cats. Although it is more difficult to protect your cat from poisonous outdoor plants because she probably enjoys roaming outside and visiting neighboring yards (gardens), you can make sure your own yard doesn't contain plants that might harm her. Some common plants to avoid include the following:

- Avocado plants
- Crocus
- Foxgloves
- Hyacinths
- Ivy
- Lilies
- Poinsettias
- Rubber plants

Poinsettia

Lily

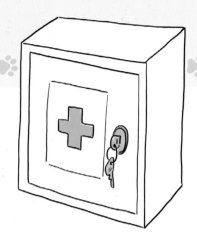

Watch out!

When your cat first arrives, you may be surprised how much she gets in your way when you are walking, winding herself around your legs. Of course, this means that she loves you, but it can be risky if you trip over your cat on the stairs or when you are carrying something. Kittens in particular are very small and quiet, so you may not realize where they are. Always be careful when closing doors in case you catch them.

Everyday products

Most cats will not try to eat or drink anything harmful, but it is advisable to keep products such as bleach and garden chemicals out of their way where they cannot knock them over. Cats get very ill and can even die if you give them human medicine such as paracetamol, or flea treatments meant for dogs. Kittens can get wrapped up in plastic bags or string, so keep an eye on them when they are playing. Luminous/glow necklaces are particularly attractive to cats—if they chew them, they can be poisoned by the chemicals.

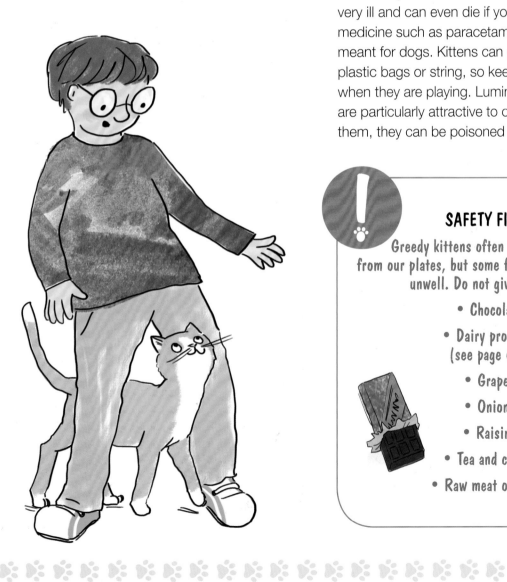

SAFETY FIRST

Greedy kittens often want to nibble from our plates, but some foods will make them unwell. Do not give your cat:

- Chocolate
- Dairy products (see page 69)
- Grapes
- Onions
- Raisins
- Tea and coffee
- Raw meat or bones

chapter 2

Getting to know your cat

When your cat arrives

The day you have been looking forward to is now here—your cat is coming home! Although you will be very excited, it is a good idea to prepare the perfect place for him before he arrives to ensure he'll be comfortable, feel relaxed, and settle into his new surroundings as quickly as possible.

The journey home

The trip to your home is likely to be your cat's first time in his cat carrier (see page 20). If you can borrow a blanket that he has already slept on and put it in his carrier, he will like the scent and it will make him feel less nervous. You could also cover his box with a light sheet or blanket to make him feel safe. (For more advice on putting your cat in his cat carrier, see page 72.)

Feline fact

Scent is extremely important for cats and they can gather lots of information from what they smell, such as where you have been and if you have touched another animal. This is because they have 40 times more scent receptors in their noses than humans.

He's home!

When you get home, open the cat carrier carefully and either lift your cat out gently or let him crawl out himself. He will immediately sniff the air to "read" his new home and become familiar with your house. Find out more about your cat's amazing sense of smell on page 53.

Create a QUIET room for YOUR CAT

Keep to one room

For the first few days, keep your cat in the same room. This will give him time to get used to the sounds and smells of his new home and also avoid him getting lost. The room should be quiet and warm, and have:

- Closed doors and windows
- Food bowls ready (try to buy the same food that he has been eating at his previous home)
- A bowl of fresh water
- A scratch post (see page 61 for how to make a simple scratch pad for your cat)
- A cat bed (see pages 24–27 for how to make a special bed for your cat)
- A safe place to hide (maybe under a bed or in a cardboard box)
- Toys
- Fresh litter in a tray

(There is more detailed information on food and litter-tray training in the next chapter.)

He is shy

Cats are usually timid in a new situation, so don't be surprised if your cat tries to hide. The most important thing you can do to reassure him is to keep your movements slow and your voice quiet, and soon he will start to trust you. Hold out your hand and softly call his name. Try not to flinch or he might be scared. If he does scuttle away into a corner or under a bed, do not pull him out but let him come out when he is ready.

Feline fact

When your cat starts to feel more confident, he may begin to wash his face and paws. This shows that he is settling in.

First night nerves

On his first night at home, your new kitten might be missing his litter-mates, so it is nice to put a hot water bottle wrapped in a blanket in his bed. The warmth will make him sleepy. Make sure he can't touch the hot water bottle directly as it may burn him. You could also do this for a new cat if you wish. Some nervous cats might like a radio left on at a low volume too. After a couple of days in his room, he can explore the rest of the house.

How to handle your cat

You might want to pick up your cat and cuddle him immediately but if you have not held a cat before, it pays to be careful. If you are a bit clumsy, he may be nervous and try to scratch you. Cats need to feel secure and safe in your arms.

You are much larger than him

Before handling your new kitten or cat, think for a minute about how he sees you. Kittens and even bigger cats will regard you as a giant, so they need to learn that you will not hurt them. It will not take long for you to become good friends as long as you remember the following:

✔ Always be kind and gentle to animals
✔ Act calmly
✔ Speak softly

Don't:

✗ Pull a cat's tail or legs
✗ Stare at your cat
✗ Put your face directly into his—he will feel scared and may lash out
✗ Interrupt him when he is eating, using his litter tray, or asleep
✗ Force him to do anything he doesn't want to do

Did you know?

Staring at your cat can make him feel threatened and uncomfortable. This is because cats will stare at other cats to scare them away.

How to pick up your cat

1 Slowly approach your cat from the side, rather than the front. Don't make any sudden movements that might alarm him.

2 Gently put one hand under his chest, behind his front legs. Put the other hand under his bottom and back legs. Lift him up carefully.

SAFETY FIRST

• Always make sure that an adult is with you for the first few times you pick up your new cat, especially if you are not used to handling cats.

• Always speak quietly and act calmly to help your cat feel relaxed.

3 Hold him against your body, but not too tightly.

4 If he shows any sign of wriggling, carefully lower him to the floor and let go when his paws touch the ground.

Feline fact

Mother cats use their mouths to gently pick up their kittens by the loose skin at the back of their necks. Don't use your hand to pick up older cats in this way because it can hurt them.

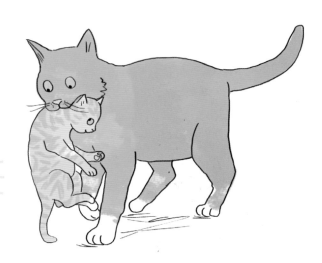

Stroking

Always use the flat of your hand to stroke your cat's back from behind his head to his tail. Do not stroke your cat in the opposite direction because this can make him feel uncomfortable.

Tickling and petting

Cats love to be tickled and played with when they are in the mood. Always make sure your cat is relaxed and happy to be touched.

✓ Try petting the back of his ears and under his chin
✗ Don't go near his tummy or face, which he might find threatening

Did you know?

The long, single strokes we give our cats remind them of their mother licking them.

FOLLOW your CAT'S lead when PLAYING

Meeting your family

When you chose your friendly kitten or cat, he was probably living with other humans, which means that he is used to having people around. Now it's time for you to introduce him to your family and any other pets. Take it slowly and let him meet the humans first.

Pleased to meet you!

Your cat will be fascinated by these new people and will want to sniff them. Make sure your family knows to keep calm and quiet. Let the cat wander around the room without being chased. There will be plenty of time to stroke, cuddle, and play with your cat once he has settled into his new home.

Swapping scents

A cat or dog that you already have in your family is likely to be jealous of your new cat or kitten, so you will need to introduce them to each other very gradually. The first stage is swapping scents. As cats and dogs are highly sensitive to smell, they need to become aware of your new cat's scent before meeting him, so gently wipe a clean cloth around your cat's whiskers and leave it in your other pet's bed. Do the same with a cloth for your other pet and put this in your new cat's bed. They will gradually accept each other's scent.

SAFETY FIRST

• If there are other animals in your house, it makes good sense to keep your new cat away from them for a couple of days. This is so that he can feel more confident in his new home before having to deal with another pet.

• Always have an adult with you when you introduce your cat to another pet in case either pet reacts badly and you need some help.

First sight

Here are some guidelines on how to introduce your new cat to different types of pets.

Meeting another cat:
• Let your cats see each other through a glass window or door first.
• The following day, wedge a door slightly open and let them sniff one another through the gap.
• When they meet in the same room, ensure each cat has an escape route in case they feel stressed or anxious.
• Hissing and miaowing is normal but do not allow them to fight—throw a blanket over them if this happens and ask an adult to take one cat out of the room.
• Keep each meeting to only a few minutes.

Meeting a dog:

- Follow the tips for another cat (see page 41) but, when your cat and dog meet properly, keep the dog on a leash (lead) and be ready to restrain the dog if he gets over-excited.
- If you introduce your cat to the dog when the dog is tired—perhaps after a long walk—your dog will be calmer and less likely to chase the newcomer. You could also try letting them meet for the first time when the dog is asleep. Your cat will, hopefully, feel like the leader of the pack from the start!
- Let the cat approach the dog.
- Don't force them together.
- Allow the cat to run away if he wants to.

Meeting small furry pets:

• Never release pet mice, guinea pigs, gerbils, or rabbits etc. from their cages when your cat is there. He may think they are food! It's important to keep your other pets safe and happy too.

Pet friends

Sometimes pets sharing a house enjoy a lovely friendship and cuddle up to sleep together, but often they avoid each other and prefer their own places. Remember that all pets need their own individual bowls and beds because sharing might cause arguments!

Feline fact

Unlike dogs, which are pack animals, cats in the wild generally live alone. So don't be surprised if your cat does not become best friends with another pet. He wants you to himself!

Your CAT may WANT YOU all to himself!

Your cat's behavior

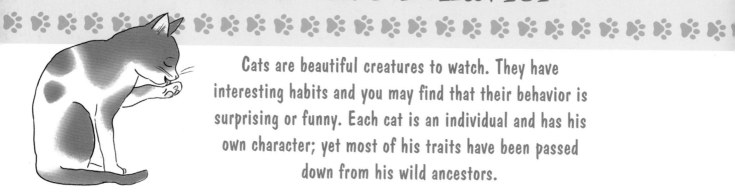

Cats are beautiful creatures to watch. They have interesting habits and you may find that their behavior is surprising or funny. Each cat is an individual and has his own character; yet most of his traits have been passed down from his wild ancestors.

Why does he do that?

All cats, including your little pet cat, originally descended from a family of wild cats thousands of years ago. Although the big cats such as lions, tigers, and lynx are much larger and more savage than domestic cats, they all share certain behaviors. Cats are expert hunters (see page 88). They are stealthy, precise, and fast at catching prey. Your cat still has these habits and occasionally you will see him act like a mini-tiger!

Feline fact

Why does your cat crouch down and wiggle his bottom before he jumps on a toy? He is preparing to pounce and, just like a runner on the starting blocks of a race, will thrust forward with his strong legs.

1 Chasing, pouncing, leaping: Your cat will enjoy chasing anything that moves—a toy or a piece of string—and will often pounce on it. It is natural even for a well-fed pet cat to play at hunting. It is good exercise for him and a fun game for you. Kittens also learn important hunting skills by playing in this way. (See Chapter 4 for fun ideas for games to play with your cat.)

Did you know?

Cats often wake up at bedtime and race around the house. This is because in the wild, they would hunt for food at dusk and dawn. So he may wake you up early in the morning too!

2 Play-biting, batting with paws: When your cat grabs your hand and pretends to bite you, he is copying what his mother taught him about catching prey (see page 89). He may also kick your hand with his back legs. If he accidentally hurts you, gently remove your hand.

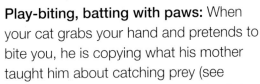

3 **Head rubbing, nudging:** Affectionate cats love to bump their heads against their owners or pieces of furniture. They also wind themselves in and out of your legs when you are trying to walk! What your cat is actually doing is leaving a scent from glands on his face on you to say he "owns" you. It's his way of saying you are his family.

4 **Kneading paws:** Kittens knead their paws on their mother's tummy to help produce more milk to drink. So when your cat kneads his paws on your lap, he is feeling contented and telling you that he is your baby!

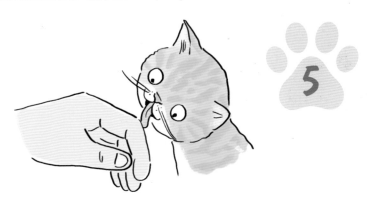

Licking: Cats are very clean animals and lick themselves regularly to clean their fur (see page 79). Licking is also a comforting habit and when cats lick you, they are grooming you as if you were one of their brothers or sisters.

SAFETY FIRST

• Always remember to wash your hands thoroughly with lots of warm water and soap if your cat has licked you, particularly before eating.

Drinking from the faucet (tap): Some cats do not drink water from their bowl but prefer to drink directly from the faucet instead. They seem to prefer the cold, running water to the stale, warm water in their bowls. Make sure you change your cat's water every day and put it somewhere away from his litter tray and food bowl. Sometimes, as a special treat, you can turn on the tap for him to have a drink! Your cat may also like to lap the raindrops from garden furniture.

Cat noises

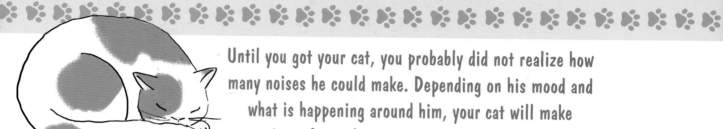

Until you got your cat, you probably did not realize how many noises he could make. Depending on his mood and what is happening around him, your cat will make a variety of sounds to try to communicate with you.

Feline fact

Cats have developed about 16 different miaow sounds around humans.

1 Miaowing

The most familiar cat noise is the miaow. Adult cats rarely miaow at each other because they can read each other's body language without making a sound, but domestic cats have learnt to miaow at their owners. He will tell you when he is hungry! (For more advice on feeding your cat to keep him fit and healthy, see pages 68–69.)

2 Purring

A cat's most restful noise is the purr, which is a vibration in the muscles of the voice box as the cat breathes. Cats mostly purr when they are contented, although, surprisingly, an ill cat may purr too. When kittens are drinking milk from their mother, they purr and she purrs back. If a kitten gets lost, he will purr as loudly as he can to alert his mother.

Did you know?

Small cats can purr but cannot roar, while big cats such as lions and tigers can roar but cannot purr. This is because of differences in their voice boxes and how much air their lungs can hold.

3 Hissing

If a cat is feeling particularly threatened, he may hiss with an open mouth to scare off the opponent and warn of a possible attack (see page 57).

4 Chirruping

A chirrup is a half-miaow that your cat uses when he is surprised to see you or if you wake him up suddenly.

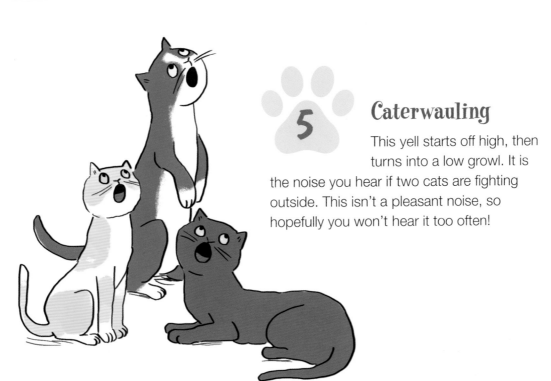

5 Caterwauling

This yell starts off high, then turns into a low growl. It is the noise you hear if two cats are fighting outside. This isn't a pleasant noise, so hopefully you won't hear it too often!

You may hear cats caterwauling AT NIGHT!

6 Chattering

You may see your cat staring out of a window at a bird when he makes this "rak-ack-ack" sound. His body will be poised to pounce, his tail lashing, and his eyes concentrated on the prey. Cats are thought to chatter when they are frustrated.

Your cat's senses

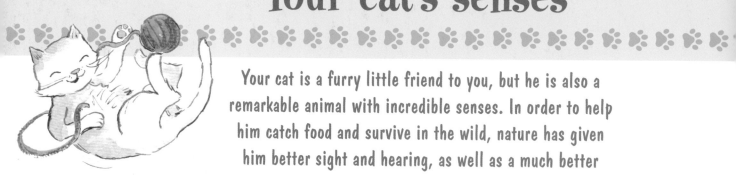

Your cat is a furry little friend to you, but he is also a remarkable animal with incredible senses. In order to help him catch food and survive in the wild, nature has given him better sight and hearing, as well as a much better sense of smell, than you.

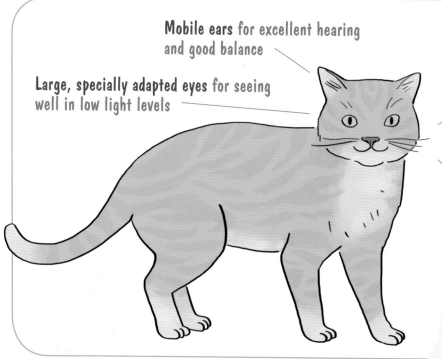

Mobile ears for excellent hearing and good balance

Large, specially adapted eyes for seeing well in low light levels

Powerful nose for sniffing out food, prey, and other cats

Sensitive whiskers for feeling his way through narrow spaces and sensing prey

Sight

Because cats naturally hunt for prey at dusk and dawn, their eyes are especially suited to seeing clearly in low light conditions. Your cat's area of perfect vision is 6½–20ft (2–6m) in front of him, so he can pounce on or run after a bird or mouse. However, he has a "blind spot" under his nose, which means that he may not immediately see a piece of food on the ground if it is too close. Although your cat does not see colors as brightly as humans do, he can detect movement without blurring better than us.

Feline fact

Have you noticed that your cat's eyes shine in the dark? This is due to a reflective layer in the back of his eyes which helps him to see better when there's not much light.

Did you know?

Cats have a third eyelid, found at the inner corner of each eye. You will usually only see it when your cat is waking up and slowly opening his eyes. If the third eyelids are very obvious, it can be a sign that your cat is ill.

Hearing

If you have seen your cat stop and stare into space, you may not realize that he is listening hard. Your cat's hearing is much better than yours. He uses his sense of hearing to locate prey very accurately and can distinguish the differences in higher-pitched sounds, such as a mouse squeak, that humans cannot hear. His large ears can turn independently in any direction to pick up distant sounds and work out exactly where they are coming from.

Feline fact

Cats have a special organ on the roof of their mouths that also helps with detecting smells. Sometimes you will see your cat using this organ when he keeps his mouth open and wrinkles his lips, gathering in a scent.

Smell

Scent is one of the most important senses for your cat. His well-trained nose is much more accurate than yours. You will notice that his first reaction to anything new is to approach it and sniff. He can tell where you have been, if you have touched another animal, and, when he checks another cat's scent in the garden, he knows its age and how long ago it visited. He will also use his scenting glands to rub against your legs and the furniture to spread his scent around his home.

Touch

Your cat's whiskers give him lots of information about his surroundings. He uses them to measure a space to see if he can squeeze through it, and also to test the temperature. If his whiskers tell him somewhere is too hot, he won't go in there! You must never cut your kitty's whiskers.

Your agile cat

Your cat is full of energy: he bounces, pounces, runs, leaps, and chases until he falls asleep! He has the powerful muscles of an athlete and the precise movements of a gymnast. You'll notice how far he can stretch and twist when washing and how tightly he can roll up into a ball when sleeping.

Cheetah

Domestic cat

Feline fact

Cats are built for speed. The cheetah can reach 60 mph (96 kmph) in three seconds. But your pet can run at up to 30 mph (48 kmph)!

Running

The cat family includes the cheetah, which is the fastest animal to run on land, and even domestic cats like yours can run at great speed. Your cat will keep his gaze focused even when he is running fast. However, his bursts of speed are short and he will soon stop to rest.

Balance

You will see your cat has a superb ability to balance on a narrow surface such as a fence. His tail helps to balance his body when jumping or climbing. Cats' spines are extremely flexible and their shoulders will squeeze into any space through which they can fit their heads.

SAFETY FIRST

• Your cat's claws may need trimming sometimes, but you should always ask an adult to do this for you or take your cat to the vet to have his claws clipped. This is important because you can really hurt your cat if you cut into the quick at the base of the claw.

• Cats can extend their claws when they need to use them to climb trees or go hunting. They can also retract them (pull them in) when they are relaxed—your cat needs to learn to do this when he is playing with you so that you don't get scratched by mistake.

Walking

If you look at your cat's muddy paw prints, you will see that they are nearly in a straight line. This means that walking on narrow ledges isn't a problem. He walks carefully, moving his right hind then right front leg forward, followed by the left hind then left front leg. He places his back paws in or near the footprints of his front paws.

Climbing

Unlike dogs, cats are expert climbers and tend to escape up a tree when threatened. Their bodies are perfectly designed for climbing, because their bones are light and they have strong muscles. Watch how your cat clings onto a tree—he can dig his very sharp claws into the bark to scamper up, although he might have more trouble coming down!

Jumping

Your cat easily leaps high and lands with no difficulty. He can jump almost six times his height. This is because of his very flexible spine and powerful leg and back muscles. Before jumping he crouches forward like a coiled spring and then quickly releases all his energy to jump to incredible heights.

Landing on their feet

Many people say that cats always land on their feet. This is usually true because their brains have developed a clever response to falling, whereby their bodies twist in the air to allow their feet to hit the ground first.

Cats' claws

Your cat's claws are made up of two layers: a white outer sheath, which is dead like your fingernails, and a pink inner "quick" that contains nerves and blood vessels. His claws grow all the time, but he keeps them short by scratching on rough surfaces such as a scratch post (see page 22).

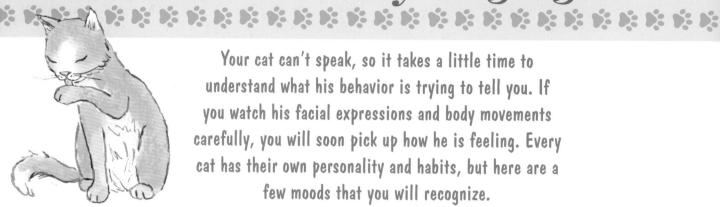
Your cat's body language

Your cat can't speak, so it takes a little time to understand what his behavior is trying to tell you. If you watch his facial expressions and body movements carefully, you will soon pick up how he is feeling. Every cat has their own personality and habits, but here are a few moods that you will recognize.

Feline fact

Your cat has his own special way of saying "hello." He stares at you, then slowly half-closes his eyes. Now you repeat the blink to say "hello" back to him!

He is relaxed

When walking, he is confident and calm. His tail is pointing straight upward and his ears are facing you. If he is lying down, his body is stretched out, his tail is flat on the ground, and his eyes may be partly closed. In this happy pose, your cat is showing that he trusts you.

What to do: Let him sniff your hand and then stroke him gently.

He is worried

If your cat is feeling nervous, he may crouch down and tense his muscles as if ready to run away. His eyes will be wide open, but try not to look directly at him, as this might scare him. His ears may be flattened or turned away from you and his tail may be close to his body. Scared cats are more likely to flee than attack.

What to do: Do not approach him, but allow him to escape and hide if he wants to.

Feline fact

Cats like to retreat to a safe hiding place, which can be under a bed or high up on a shelf. This behavior is like a wild cat climbing up a tree to escape danger.

He is angry

A cat that feels threatened will try to defend himself by appearing aggressive. He may arch his back and his fur may stand on end. His eyes will be narrowed and his ears will be flattened and pulled far back on his head. He may show his teeth and even hiss. A lashing tail is always a sign of annoyance. When his front paw is raised, he is ready to hit out, so keep well away.

What to do: Never make an angry cat more frightened by shouting at or touching him. Instead, keep quiet and move away.

Let's not fight!

Cats have clever ways of scaring cats or other animals that are threatening them. Their fur stands up to make them look larger and they often walk in a sideways manner to seem more dangerous. A hard stare can see off their rival before a fight even begins.

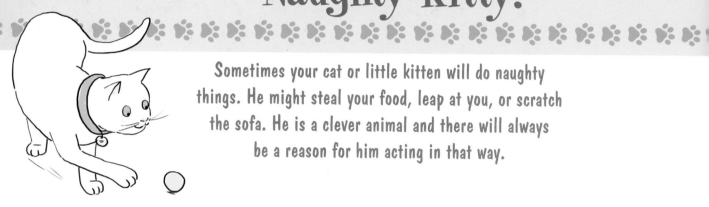

Naughty kitty!

Sometimes your cat or little kitten will do naughty things. He might steal your food, leap at you, or scratch the sofa. He is a clever animal and there will always be a reason for him acting in that way.

Don't do that!

All pets are individuals and have their own character. Your cat might be peskier than most, but it is good to try to see things from his perspective. If something makes him feel nervous, he may be lashing out as a defence.

What might upset him?

- **Noise:** Cats have very sensitive ears, so your loud music or the vacuum cleaner and washing machine will sound very loud to him.
- **Being disturbed while eating:** Food is essential for him and he will not like being interrupted.
- **Stroking his tummy:** Some cats dislike being tickled in vulnerable areas such as the tummy.
- **Other pets/dogs:** He may have had a fright when a dog barked at him and now does not want to go outside.
- **Boredom:** Cats need exercise and play.

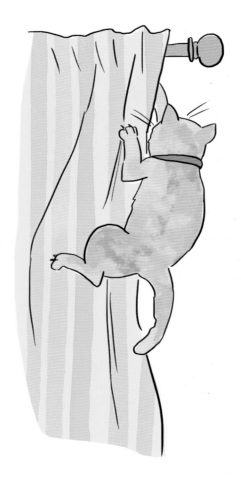

How he may react

Here are some of the ways your cat may behave if he is feeling upset or bored:

• Pouncing
• Trying to bite or scratch
• Hissing
• Hiding away
• Climbing
• Not being friendly

Reasons why

Cats need plenty of stimulation and affection. If your cat isn't getting enough play-time with you, he might be trying to get your attention by being naughty. If he is feeling ignored, perhaps because there is a new pet in the house, he may also be badly behaved. If he is racing around and leaping on the drapes (curtains), he may need more time in the garden.

Try to PLAY with your cat every day

What to do

- If he is being aggressive, ignore him and leave the room.
- Never hit or harm him.
- Never force him out of his hiding place.
- Tell him "no" firmly.
- Don't encourage bad habits by allowing your cat to climb on work surfaces, scratch sofas, or play-bite your fingers.
- Talk to him in a calm voice.
- Play with him every day.
- Make sure he goes outside to exercise each day.
- Be kind and give him cat treats when he is calm and friendly (although not too many as they may make him put on weight).

However, be aware that if his habits change a lot and he becomes very shy, doesn't want to eat, or licks himself over and over, he may be unwell. If so, you will need to take him to see the vet (see pages 75–77).

Make a scratching pad

To stop your cat scratching the furniture, why not make him a scratching pad of his own? He will love using his claws on the exposed cardboard edges!

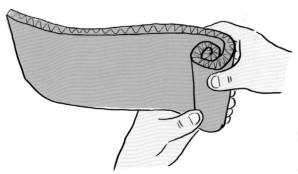

1 Cut some long strips from a cardboard box and start curling them up into a spiral. Secure the end of the first strip with some sticky tape.

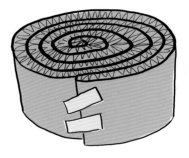

2 Keep wrapping the strips around the pad until it reaches the size you want. Secure the final strip with more sticky tape.

3 To make it easier for your cat to scratch at the pad, thread a piece of string through a gap in the center, tie a firm knot, and hang the pad from a door handle.

Kitten behaviors

Young cats and kittens need more training than older cats because they are lively and curious. While this is charming—and sometimes fun— your kitten needs to be taught good behavior. You may find that he:

- Climbs on worktops and the dining table
- Scratches furniture
- Knocks over objects
- Tries to eat your food
- Play-bites

Always be patient with your kitten. Say "no" when he is misbehaving and move him away from the problem. It may take a few weeks, but he will soon learn to be a good cat!

10 amazing cat facts

Here are 10 fascinating facts about cats so you can impress your friends with your cat knowledge.

1

Cats do not have tastebuds for sweet flavors, which means that they cannot taste sweet foods.

2 **Owning a cat can keep you healthier.** Stroking your pet cat can make you feel calmer and even slow down your heart rate. So, if you are feeling angry or upset about something, go and have a cuddle with your cat!

3 Kittens are born with blue eyes, but the color may change as they get older. This is also true of humans, although adult cats' eyes have a wider color range. They can have blue, green, brown, or yellow-colored eyes.

4 In ancient Egypt, when a pet cat died, the owners would show their sadness by shaving off their eyebrows. Around 4,000 years ago, the ancient Egyptians began to encourage wild cats into their villages in order to keep down the number of rats and mice, which were destroying their crops. Cats became so important to the Egyptian people that they worshipped a cat goddess called Bast or Bastet.

5 Cats' eyes are very large compared to their heads; they are almost as big as human eyes, although their heads are much smaller than ours. Although they have excellent long sight, cats have a "blind spot" near their nose. To make up for this, they use their whiskers to sense objects close to their face (see page 53).

Tiger   Wild cat

6 There is a type of wild cat on every continent, apart from Australia and Antarctica. The 37 surviving species of wild cat have spread around the world. These include lions in Africa, pumas in America, tigers in Asia, and wild cats in Europe. The largest wild cat is the tiger, while the smallest is the African black-footed cat.

7 Most cats have five toes on their front paws and four toes on their hind paws. The extra front claws help cats to climb trees and catch prey. However, some cats have more toes than this—as many as eight toes on one foot! They are called polydactyl cats and inherit this difference from their parents or grandparents. The record for the cat with the most toes is 28!

8 A male cat is called a Tom and a female cat is known as a Queen.

9 **Cats can only sweat through their paws.** Cats are much less sensitive to changes in temperature than humans, but on a hot day you may see a cat rolling around on the ground to cool down and spot little damp paw-prints from their sweaty paws!

10

The ridges on each cat's nose are unique—like a human's fingerprint. Cats say hello to each other by touching noses.

Stroking your cat can make you feel **HAPPY**

chapter 3
Everyday care

The right food

Your cat needs the correct type of food to stay fit and healthy. There is a large choice of cat and kitten food available in grocery and pet stores, so you may have to experiment to find out which is the best for your pet.

What cats like to eat

All cats, big and small, are carnivores, which means they only eat meat. Cats depend on meat to provide essential nutrients. In the wild, for example, lions and cheetahs catch prey such as antelope and zebra, while small cats catch and eat prey like birds and mice. Don't give your cat leftovers from your plate, as some human food is poisonous to cats (see page 29). You can give her occasional cat treats, but not too many!

SAFETY FIRST

• Never give dog food to your cat. It does not contain enough nutrients for cats and may make her ill.

• Cats that do not eat meat become seriously ill. Do not feed your cat a vegan or vegetarian diet.

Dry or wet food?

You should look for cat food that says "complete" on the label. This means that the food contains all the nutrients your cat needs, although it is nice to give her some ham or tuna fish as a treat now and then.

Either dry or wet cat food is fine to give your kitty. Wet food comes in pouches or tins. If wet food is left in your cat's bowl, it will become smelly and attract flies. Dry food is packaged in boxes or bags. It can be measured out more easily than wet food, which can help you keep track of how much your pet is eating, but you will need to provide more water for her to drink. She will soon let you know which type of food she prefers!

Kitten and cat food

You can buy specially formulated kitten food that is suitable for cats up to 12 months old. Then you can move your kitten on to adult cat food.

Feline fact

Don't be surprised if you see your cat eating grass and being a little sick afterward. When cats groom themselves hair gets caught on their rough tongues. They then swallow the hair, which builds up into a fur ball in their stomach. Cats use grass to make themselves sick so they can get rid of the fur ball and also any bits of bones or fur they might have swallowed when eating prey.

How much and when?

Kittens up to the age of 4 months need five to six small meals each day. From 6 months old, cats need two to three bigger portions every day.

Feed your cat at roughly the same time each day—cats like routine and will complain loudly if you forget! Call your cat's name and give her the food in a clean bowl. Always leave your pet alone to eat. It is sensible for one person in the family to be responsible for feeding; otherwise your cat might eat too many meals!

Water or milk?

Although cats often enjoy drinking milk (and eating dairy products such as yogurt and cheese), many can get upset stomachs as a result, so these are best avoided. You can buy specialty cat milk from pet and grocery stores, but perhaps save this as a treat for your cat, as it is expensive. The best drink for your cat is fresh water, which you should provide in a clean bowl every day. You may find that your cat prefers to drink from a dripping faucet (see page 47) or even lap from a rain puddle!

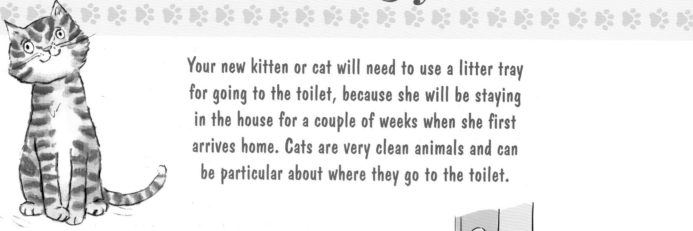

Toilet-training your cat

Your new kitten or cat will need to use a litter tray for going to the toilet, because she will be staying in the house for a couple of weeks when she first arrives home. Cats are very clean animals and can be particular about where they go to the toilet.

Why does she need a litter tray?

There are two reasons why your cat will need a litter tray (see page 22), at least to begin with. Firstly, it's a good idea to keep a cat indoors for the first 14 days after she arrives so that she can get used to her new home and family, and also spread her scent around (which she does to mark out her territory). The other reason is that kittens cannot go out into the yard (garden) until two weeks after their 12-week immunizations (see page 73). So your cat will need somewhere to go to the toilet until she is allowed outside.

SAFETY FIRST

• Litter trays are full of germs, so it's important that they are cleaned thoroughly every day. However, you should ask an adult to do this for you. If you touch the tray, always wash your hands carefully with soap and hot water.

How to toilet-train your cat

It is likely that your kitten or cat has already used a litter tray in her previous home but, if not, don't worry, as it won't take long for her to learn what to do. Bear in mind that even if she is familiar with litter trays, she may need reminding how to use one in her new home.

1 Use a large plastic tray—some of these have a lid, which your kitten may prefer since it means she can go to the toilet in private. Place the tray near the back door on some newspaper because when cats dig in the litter they can scatter it over the side and make a mess.

2 Fill the tray with cat litter (which you can buy from grocery or pet stores and the vet). Try to use the same litter that your kitten is familiar with from her previous home.

3 After your kitten has eaten, pick her up and gently place her in the tray. You will need to do this after every meal to make sure she understands that it's time to go to the toilet!

4 Give your kitten lots of praise when she uses the tray, but don't scold her when she makes a mistake. You may find an older cat adapts more quickly to her new litter tray than a little kitten that has only recently been toilet-trained.

First visit to the vet

Now you are responsible for an animal, you must register her at the local veterinary surgery. The vet is the person you will visit to ask for advice or when your cat needs medical care.

How to put your cat in a carrier

Many cats don't enjoy being placed in their cat carriers. Here is a helpful technique that should make this much easier:

1 Wrap your cat in a thick towel first of all, so that she feels warm and safe. The towel will also stop her wiggling and make it easier to lift her up.

2 Slide your cat into her carrier, bottom-first. You can buy a special spray that contains calming scents for the carrier, which can make your cat feel less nervous.

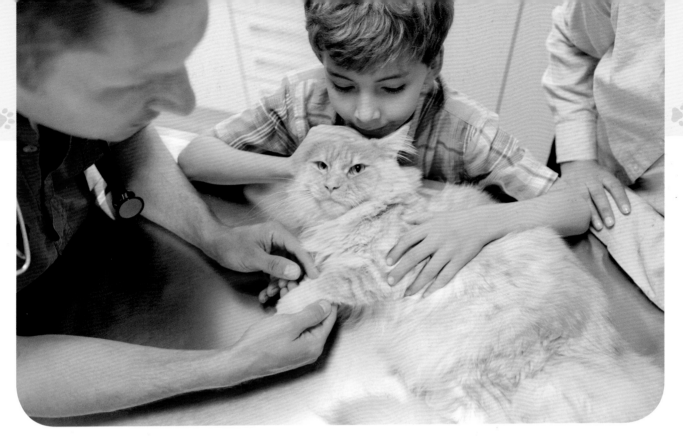

SAFETY FIRST

• If your cat is injured in some way, then you may find that she hides from you. Injured cats are also more likely to scratch or bite because they are in pain, so it's best to ask an adult to deal with your cat if she is hurt.

Meeting the vet

On her first visit to the vet, your cat will be checked all over to make sure she is healthy. Her temperature will be taken, her teeth looked at, and she will be weighed. The vet will also use a stethoscope to listen to her heart and lungs and check she is well. This is a good time to ask the vet any questions you may have about how to care for your pet.

Immunizations

Kittens are given injections to protect them from certain diseases when they are 8–9 weeks old and again at 12 weeks old. The vet will tell you how long to keep your kitty inside following her immunizations—this is usually 14 days. You will also need to take your cat back to the vet every year for a "booster" injection, which keeps the protection strong.

Treating fleas

Fleas can live in your cat's fur and make her itchy. They can also bite humans so if someone in your household has lots of itchy bites, check your cat for fleas. The vet will give you a liquid treatment that is squeezed onto the back of the neck to kills the fleas. Ask an adult to apply it following the instructions given. Your vet will recommend applying a treatment regularly (the frequency depends on the product) to stop your cat getting fleas. There are also cat collars that contain a flea treatment, but these don't work as well as the liquid. Flea treatments are also available as tablets. If your cat has fleas, treat your house with a special spray.

SAFETY FIRST

• Once the flea treatment has been applied, do not touch the area until it has dried. If you do accidentally touch it, wash your hands thoroughly. Do not put your hands near your mouth.

• Never use dog flea treatments on your cat. They include an ingredient that is dangerously toxic to cats.

Treating worms

Worms live inside cats and can make them ill. Your cat may pick up worms when she eats a bird or mouse. Worms can come out of your cat in her poo and also make people very ill. For this reason, you should never touch cat poo with your bare hands. Always wash your hands with soap and hot water as quickly as possible if you touch poo by mistake. You can use a cat worming medicine to get rid of the worms. The vet will pop a tablet in your cat's mouth, which destroys them. You can buy these medicines from the vet for you to use at home. There are also liquid treatments for worms, which are applied like the flea treatments.

Microchipping

It is a good idea to have your pet microchipped. This means asking the vet to insert a tiny microchip under her skin which contains details of your address, just in case she ever goes missing. If someone finds her, the vet can use a special scanner to read the chip and will then be able to contact you.

Neutering

In the past there used to be lots of stray cats because of kittens being born that no one wanted. Nowadays, vets recommend that cats have a small operation so that they do not have kittens. An adult will organize this with the vet when your cat is around 4 months old. The operation is different for female and male cats. For females it is called spaying and for male cats it is called castration.

Keeping your cat healthy

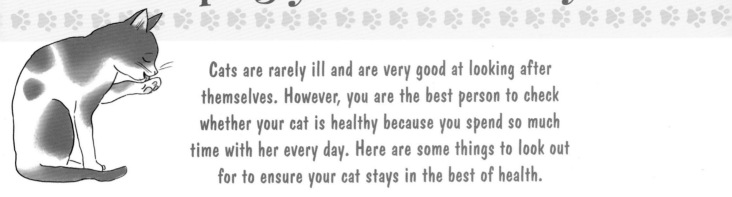

Cats are rarely ill and are very good at looking after themselves. However, you are the best person to check whether your cat is healthy because you spend so much time with her every day. Here are some things to look out for to ensure your cat stays in the best of health.

1 General behavior

If your cat suddenly does not want to be handled—and yowls or miaows when you touch her—she may have an injury such as a sore leg or perhaps a thorn in her paw. Another common symptom of illness is when your cat doesn't want to eat her food. She may have a tummy upset or a sore mouth.

2 Eyes

Your cat's eyes should be wide open and clear. There should not be any gooey discharge. If her third eyelid is constantly visible (see page 53), then she may be unwell.

3 Ears

Be sure that your cat's ears are moving normally and that she doesn't flinch when you touch them. If she does, she may have ear mites, which are little insects that live in her ears and make her scratch.

Feline fact

Did you know that cats can have dandruff? Dandruff shows as tiny white flakes of skin in your cat's fur. If your cat has dark fur, dandruff will show more, but it is not usually a problem. However, if it gets worse and your cat's fur has lost its shine, or if she is scratching a lot, then it is best to talk to the vet about it.

4 Coat

Your pet's coat should feel clean and look shiny, without any roughness or patches of baldness. If she is scratching a lot, then she may have fleas (see page 74). If she is not grooming herself, it may be a sign that she is ill or in pain.

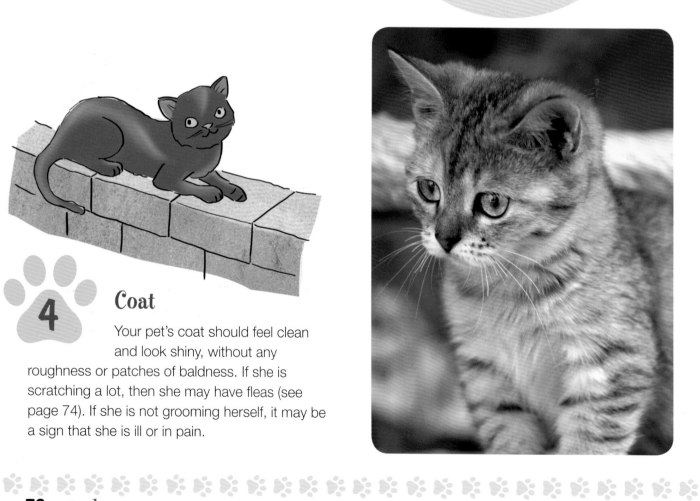

5 Teeth

Your cat's teeth should be white, without too much staining, and her gums should be pink, not an angry red color. Cats' breath can be a bit smelly after they have eaten but if her breath is terrible, she may have a problem with her teeth. Visit your vet to find out if anything is wrong. Be careful when you look at your cat's teeth, especially if she isn't used to having this done. Make sure an adult is with you when you do this.

6 Bottom

If there is any poo around your cat's bottom, she may have diarrhea and need to be taken to the vet to be checked properly.

SAFETY FIRST

• If you think your cat isn't well in any way, or if she has had an accident, then tell an adult and ask him or her to phone the vet immediately for advice.

• Always make sure an adult comes with you to any appointments with the vet.

Good grooming

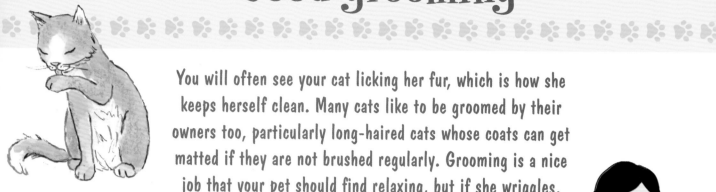

You will often see your cat licking her fur, which is how she keeps herself clean. Many cats like to be groomed by their owners too, particularly long-haired cats whose coats can get matted if they are not brushed regularly. Grooming is a nice job that your pet should find relaxing, but if she wriggles, always let her run away. You won't need to give your cat a bath because most cats don't like getting wet.

1 Use a special cat brush or latex (rubber) cat comb to groom your cat. A box of tissues will be useful for collecting loose hairs.

2 You can groom your cat by kneeling next to her on the floor or stand her on a table if this is easier. You could also sit on a chair with your cat on your lap. Start by stroking her gently to make her feel calm and sleepy.

3 Using the cat brush, hold your cat gently and then carefully stroke her fur from neck to tail.

4 Brush her legs and tail in turn. You may need to ask an adult to help you hold her while you are brushing.

Rough tongues

Cats' tongues are covered in rough, backward-facing barbs that pull away any dirt from their fur as they lick and wash themselves. This roughness also helps them detangle their fur and rasp meat from prey when they are eating. You will feel how rough your cat's tongue is when she licks you.

5 Collect up any loose hair and then put this in a tissue. You can throw it in the trash can (dustbin) later.

SAFETY FIRST

• Always have an adult with you when you groom your cat.

• Always avoid sensitive areas such as your cat's face and tummy.

6 You may notice black specks that look like dirt near your cat's skin or in the fur you have groomed out. This is flea poo and means your cat needs a flea treatment (see page 74).

7 After your cat's grooming session, it is nice to reward her, so give her a treat and let her go. Your cat will hopefully come to enjoy being groomed and it will help her to bond with you too.

When your cat goes outside

A cat will have been kept indoors for a couple of weeks since arriving at her new home, while a kitten has had to stay inside following her 12-week immunizations (see page 73). Whether you have a cat or kitten, it's now time for her to start exploring her new outdoor surroundings or to experience the outside world for the first time. Although she may appear nervous, her instinct will soon lead her to investigate the sights and sounds of your yard (garden).

First time out

1 You may want your kitten or cat to wear a harness and leash (lead) for her first few visits outside so you can keep a loose hold of her and be certain that she won't run off. It is a good idea to buy an adjustable harness to ensure it fits your kitten or cat properly. Try the harness on her at home a couple of days before her first visit outdoors to give her a chance to get used to the feel of it around her body.

2 Walk out of the door with your cat and gently encourage her to trot along with you. Let her set the pace and go as slowly as she wants.

SAFETY FIRST

• Put a collar with an address tag on your cat in case she gets lost (see page 23) or get her microchipped.

• If you want to use a harness on an older cat, make sure you have an adult with you when you first use it.

Your cat loves to EXPLORE outdoors!

 **3** Let your cat sniff all the smells—they will be fascinating to her and tell her who has passed through the yard—and watch the birds.

SAFETY FIRST

• Cats and kittens should be locked in at night to minimize the chance of a car accident. Doing this also helps protect wildlife from your hunter cat. Mice, voles, shrews, and other rodents are more likely to be out and about at night.

• Don't worry if your cat doesn't come back for a while when you let her out. She will eventually come home, especially if she is hungry.

4 Keep the first outing to about five minutes, then increase to around ten minutes the next day.

5 After a couple of days, you can let your cat out without the harness. Stay close by and keep an eye on her. Leave the back door open so that she can return when she wants to.

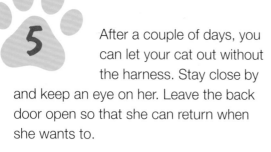

6 It is best to let your cat out when she is hungry, so that she will come home more quickly for her food! Call your cat's name and rattle her food in a bowl until she appears. Give her a treat and lots of cuddles when she comes home.

Feline fact

Cats are highly territorial animals, which means that they stick to a particular territory (your yard and perhaps a neighbor's too). They will leave their scent in this area to warn any other cats that they "own" that patch. Most arguments between cats are because of territories.

Cat-flap training

Once your kitten or cat is used to going outside, it is time to teach her how to use a cat flap. A cat flap is a small door that fits into the back door or in a hole in a wall. Your cat will be able to let herself in and out of the house without bothering you.

Why use a cat flap?

Cats are independent animals that, unlike dogs, like to do their own thing. They decide when they want to explore the yard (garden), have some exercise, chase a bird, or go out to the toilet. A cat flap allows them to leave and return when they wish.

Did you know?

Depending on their personality, some cats like to be outdoors for long periods of time, while others enjoy being at home. You may find that your cat wants to come back in again just after you've let her out. This could be because cats like to come indoors to eat a "mouseful" of food before going outside again to explore.

Which type of cat flap?

Cat flaps have a little transparent flap that moves back and forward to let your cat in and out of the house. Some models have a memory button that remembers a tag on your cat's collar and will only let her in. You can also buy cat flaps that recognize your pet's microchip and will only open for her. This is useful because no local cats can come in and eat your kitty's food! All cat flaps are lockable.

Teaching your cat to use a cat flap

1 Lift the flap and prop it open with a stick so that it does not move. Make sure the stick is secure, as you don't want the flap to shut suddenly and frighten your cat while you're training her.

2 Leaving your cat inside, go outside and hold a cat treat (or some dry food) through the opening.

3 Call your cat and encourage her to walk through. If at first she doesn't respond, give her lots more encouragement and keep trying.

4 When your cat walks through the cat flap, reward her with a treat.

5 Repeat this process in the opposite direction so that she learns how to come back into the house.

6 When your cat is more confident, take the stick away and show her with your hand how to push open the flap.

7 Continue to reward your cat with a treat when she manages to get through the cat flap all by herself!

Your little hunter

Your cat loves to be outside in the fresh air, running and leaping about. Although she is well fed at home, she will spend much of her time chasing and hunting small prey outdoors. This is a natural instinct that your cat learnt as a kitten.

Why does she hunt?

Your little cat is the product of thousands of years of breeding. She is closely related to big cats such as lions, tigers, and cheetahs which all share her hunting skills. All cats are designed to catch smaller animals to eat for dinner.

Did you know?

Cats have fur between the soft pads of their paws to silence their walking as they stalk prey.

Lion hunting

Domestic cat stalking

How does she hunt?

If you watch your cat, you will notice that she often tries to chase other creatures such as bees and butterflies. First, she will fix her gaze on the prey, crouch down, and hide, then she will focus on it and pounce! Mostly, she will not catch anything, but play-hunting is good exercise for her.

What does she hunt?

Some cats are not very successful at catching prey, but others become excellent hunters. Kittens often start catching and eating flies and worms before moving on to larger creatures such as birds, mice, and shrews. If there is a handy fish pond nearby, you may see her eating a goldfish.

Yuck! What's that?

Unfortunately, one unpleasant aspect of owning a cat is finding a dead mouse or bird on the floor. Although you may find this horrible, it's no use telling your cat off. In her mind, she has presented you with a wonderful, fresh meal that she caught just for you. When she was a kitten, her mother brought home a bird or mouse to feed her and now your cat is repeating the honor for you!

What to do: Don't touch the "present" your cat has brought home. Instead, ask an adult to wrap it in some newspaper and put it in a garbage can (dustbin) outside. Then it's important to wash the area where your cat dropped the prey.

Bird alert!

If you would like to prevent your cat catching birds, then try fitting a bell to her collar. The sudden tinkling of the bell will alert the bird in her sights and give it a chance to fly away.

SAFETY FIRST

• If your cat does catch prey, she may pick up fleas and worms from the creatures she has caught, so you must always ensure her flea treatments and worm tablets are up-to-date (see page 74).

• If your cat brings home live prey, such as a bird or mouse, then ask an adult to help you.

chapter 4
Your cat as playmate

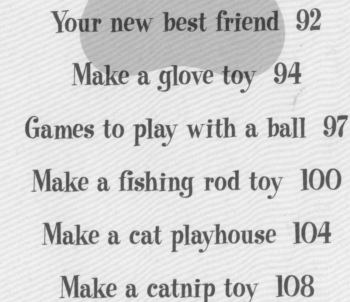

Your new best friend

Your cat is going to be your new best friend. He'll be a willing playmate and is sure to enjoy your attention and playing games with you. Both kittens and cats love to play, but kittens will need some rest afterward!

SAFETY FIRST

• Always be careful not to get too close to your cat's claws, as you may get scratched accidentally.

• Keep plastic bags away from your pet in case he gets tangled up.

• When a game is over, always put away toys that use string, ribbon, shoelaces, or yarn (wool) because your cat can swallow these.

• Laser light toys are not recommended because they are frustrating for your cat and can be dangerous for your own eyes.

• Don't use your fingers as toys, even under blankets or clothes—the cute little kitten that playfully bites them will soon grow up into a cat with much bigger teeth!

Why do cats like to play?

Cats are intelligent animals, and need play and exercise to keep them physically fit and mentally alert. Most of their play is mock-hunting—they will leap, pounce, and race around crazily. Your cat's mother taught him how to chase and jump on a mouse and he is simply copying this behavior when he plays with a toy. There will be many times when you find your cat's antics make you laugh, and playing together will also help strengthen the friendship you have.

Did you know?

Cats have extra whiskers just above their paws on the back of their front legs. They use them to sense the prey they have caught.

What do cats enjoy doing?

- Rolling and chasing toys such as balls
- Leaping on toys such as feathers on a stick
- Spotting anything that moves unexpectedly
- Finding anything partly hidden such as a toy under a cloth
- Being in small spaces, perhaps by squashing themselves into a cupboard or den
- Being high up and perhaps batting your hair from above!
- Teasing games such as "now you see it, now you don't"
- Playing with boxes as they love to jump out and surprise you!
- Playing with paper (for example, they enjoy sitting on it)

Having fun together

There are so many games you can play together and your cat will amaze you with his fantastic jumping and pouncing skills. Not all cats enjoy the same things, however, so if he isn't too interested in one particular toy, then just try something else. For example, you could roll a small ball past your cat's paws and see if he follows it. You could also throw a ball of yarn (wool) into the air and he may leap up to catch it. Perhaps let him see a toy and then slowly hide it—he'll be fascinated. When you're teasing your cat with a toy, let him capture it sometimes or he may give up.

There are lots of exciting games and activities for you to try out with your cat in this chapter.

Make a glove toy

You know that your cat is fantastic at jumping, so why not make him a special toy out of things you already have around the house? Find an old glove, some spare yarn (wool) or shoelaces, and some little cat toys, and you'll be able to make a fun toy that you'll both enjoy playing with.

You will need

Scissors

Yarn/wool (you could also use some string or old shoelaces)

Toy mouse, colorful feathers, and other small cat toys

An old glove (preferably made from yarn/wool)

1 Cut five lengths of yarn (wool), so that each piece is about 20in (50cm) long.

2 Tie a small cat toy to the end of each piece of yarn (wool) that you know your cat will like to catch. You could try using a toy mouse, a little ball of yarn, or perhaps some colorful feathers.

Did you know?

Cats are excellent at jumping. In 2013, a cat named Alley from Chicago, USA, created the world record for the longest cat jump. She jumped a distance of 72in (182.88cm)!

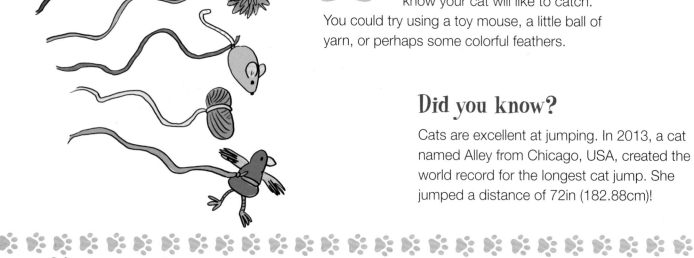

Cats love to BAT AT dangling objects!

3 Put your hand in the glove and ask an adult or friend to wrap the other end of the first piece of yarn (wool) around one of the fingertips. Tie a couple of knots so that the yarn is nice and secure, but not too tightly because you will need to put the glove on and take it off again.

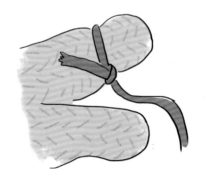

4 Repeat Step 3 for the other four fingertips.

SAFETY FIRST

• Your cat will be excited when playing this game, so be careful that he doesn't catch your hand with his claws.

• Always put the glove toy away when the game is over because your cat might get tangled up in the yarn (wool).

5 Put on the glove, hold up your hand, and then move your fingers up and down to make the toys move. Watch your cat leap up to try to reach the dangling toys!

Games to play with a ball

With his lightning-quick reactions, your pet cat cannot resist playing with a ball. Try out these ball games to see which one he enjoys playing the most. You may discover that he is a feline David Beckham!

1

Football

If you have a small soft ball—or an old ball of yarn (wool)—kick it near to your cat (but not directly at his face). He may bat at it with his paws and even dribble it across the floor. When it is your turn, gently nudge it past him and see if you can score more goals than him!

SAFETY FIRST

- With any ball game, make sure that you use a ball that is not small enough for your cat to put in his mouth. A ping-pong ball is a good size. Never use marbles or similarly small balls as these might choke him.

2

Ping-pong

A simple game to play, which many cats love, is bouncing a ping-pong ball. It is best to play this game on a hard floor, such as a kitchen floor, so that the ball bounces high into the air. Most cats will try to knock the ball down to the ground.

Did you know?

Scientists have studied cats to see if they are right-pawed or left-pawed. Most cats seem to be ambidextrous (i.e. happy to use either paw) to do simple things, but some of them prefer to use either their right or left paw for more difficult tasks. Why not watch your cat when he is playing with a ball and see if he is right-pawed, left-pawed, or ambidextrous?

SAFETY FIRST
• Never throw a ball (or any other toy) directly at your cat's face. It may frighten him. Try rolling the ball just to the side of him and watch him pounce!

3 Water play

Let's see if your cat likes water! Find a large plastic bowl and fill it nearly to the top with water—make sure this isn't too cold. Add a few ping-pong balls to the water and move them around. Will your cat try to bat the bobbing balls with his paws or nudge them with his nose?

4 Find the ball

Get some cardboard tubes, such as used toilet roll tubes, and cut them into equal-sized sections. Find an empty tissue box, cut out the top with some scissors, and stand it on one of the long sides. Then stack the sections of tube one on top of the other inside the box. Place a small ball in one of the tubes and see if your cat tries to pull it out with his dextrous paws. A few cat treats or dry food might encourage him!

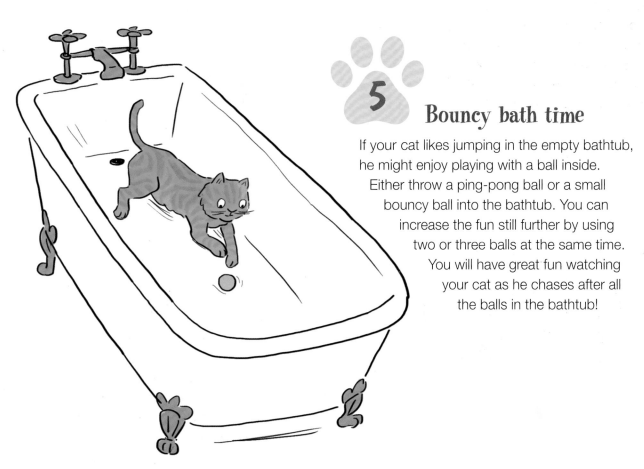

5 Bouncy bath time

If your cat likes jumping in the empty bathtub, he might enjoy playing with a ball inside. Either throw a ping-pong ball or a small bouncy ball into the bathtub. You can increase the fun still further by using two or three balls at the same time. You will have great fun watching your cat as he chases after all the balls in the bathtub!

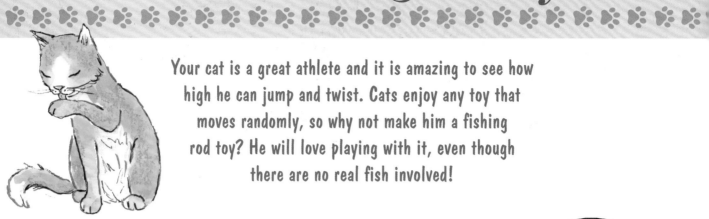

Make a fishing rod toy

Your cat is a great athlete and it is amazing to see how high he can jump and twist. Cats enjoy any toy that moves randomly, so why not make him a fishing rod toy? He will love playing with it, even though there are no real fish involved!

You will need

Yarn (wool) or string

A stick (e.g. a cane, stick, or chopstick), at least 12in (30cm) long

Scissors

Feathers, ribbons or shoelaces, and small cat toys

1 Cut a piece of yarn (wool) or string to a length of about 20in (50cm).

2 Take the stick and tie the long piece of yarn (wool) or string to it, about 4in (10cm) from one end. Make sure you knot the yarn a few times so it's secure.

3 Tie some feathers to the other end of the piece of yarn (wool) or string. Ensure the knot is nice and tight.

4 You can make extra tails for your cat to play with by cutting smaller lengths of yarn (wool) and tying them together in the center with a spare piece of yarn.

Feline fact

Kittens are programmed from birth to chase and catch things. They will chase anything that moves—even their mother's flicking tail!

5 Tie the bundle of tails to the main piece of yarn (wool) or string. If you wish, you can tie a couple of bundles to the toy for added interest.

6 Tie the other objects you've collected to the piece of yarn (wool) or string, making sure you space them out evenly so your cat can bat at each one. He will be attracted to ribbons or shoelaces—in fact, anything that dangles! You could also attach small cat toys such as a little mouse to the yarn or string.

SAFETY FIRST

• Cats love to bite and pull at the yarn (wool) or string and toys, so watch that your pet doesn't try to eat any part of the fishing rod toy. Also be careful of the end of the stick, which may be sharp.

• Do not attach anything to the fishing rod, such as a small ball, bell, or pompom, that is small enough to choke your pet.

7 Call your kitty and hold the stick up high, moving it back and forth. Is your cat interested? If not, lower the stick and trail the wool (yarn) or string and toys along the floor, then lift it up when he tries to grab it. Have fun!

Make a cat playhouse

Cats and kittens often hide in small spaces and jump out to surprise you. If you have an old cardboard box, you could make a little house for your pet. He will be keen to go inside and explore the doors and windows.

You will need

....

An old cardboard box

Strong parcel tape

A pencil

Scissors

Paint and paintbrush or marker pens

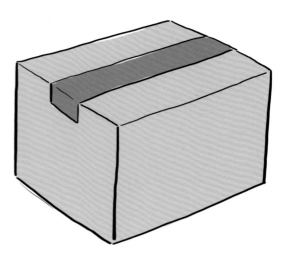

 **1** Take your cardboard box and tape together the flaps on the top of the box. Make sure the tape is pushed down firmly so that the box does not come apart while your cat is playing inside.

2 Draw some shapes on the outside of the box to cut out as windows. These can be any shape you like, but make sure they are large enough for your cat to peep out of or walk through. You could try cutting out circles in different sizes (as shown here) or perhaps a door and some proper windows to create a little cat house. You might even like to cut out a cat's head shape for your cat to jump through.

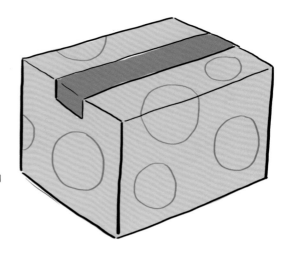

3 Cut out the different shapes with the scissors. Be careful of your fingers and ask an adult for help if you find it difficult to cut through the thick cardboard.

Watch your cat **JUMP** in and out of the box!

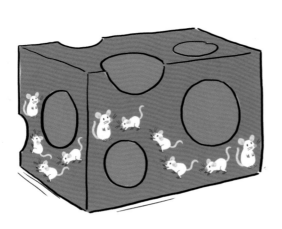 

4 Now paint your cat playhouse or decorate it with some drawings. Paint it in a bright color and then add a line of little mice or perhaps a trail of cat paw-prints. You could try adding details such as drapes (curtains) and plants around the windows and door if you've turned the box into a proper cat house.

5 Your cat's playhouse is now finished. Encourage him inside with one of his favorite toys or some dry food. He will soon get used to his new toy and enjoy jumping in and out of the holes.

Feline fact

Cats and kittens like cardboard because it is warm to sit on. It's also a very good material for them to practice sharpening their claws on! You could also try putting some old newspapers inside the playhouse for your cat to ruffle up.

Variation

If you have more than one cardboard box, try joining them together to make a longer box or tape one on top of the other to build a high-rise apartment for your lucky cat.

Make a catnip toy

Lots of cats like playing with toys that contain catnip. Catnip is a plant with a scent that many cats go crazy for. They roll in it, jump around, and get excited. You can buy dried catnip in bags at pet stores. Try making a catnip toy and see if your cat enjoys it too.

You will need

An old sock

Cotton wool or an old pair of pantyhose (tights)

Dried catnip

1 Open the sock and fill it half-way up with cotton wool. You could also use some soft padding material such as your mum's old pantyhose (tights)!

SAFETY FIRST

• If your cat is one of those who loves catnip, watch out in case he gets a bit too excited. Occasionally, a cat might become aggressive around catnip, so keep your hands clear when he is playing with this toy.

Feline fact

Only about 40 percent of cats react to catnip. This is because a preference for catnip is a genetic reaction that these cats have inherited from their parents. Cats who like catnip will begin to notice its scent from the age of about 3 months.

2 Put some dried catnip inside the sock—a couple of teaspoons should be enough.

3 Tie the open end of the sock into a firm knot.

Feline fact

It seems that not only domestic cats like catnip, but some of their larger cousins do too. In tests, lions, leopards, jaguars, and lynx reacted strongly to the plant, but tigers not so much!

4 Let your cat sniff at the sock. Does he look interested? Your cat will get very excited if he likes the catnip. If he doesn't like the smell, then perhaps you could give the catnip sock to a friend with a cat to try out instead.

Variation

To make your catnip sock even more fascinating for your pet, insert some crinkly candy wrappers or perhaps a small bell when you are filling it with cotton wool. He will hear the sound, but won't be able to eat the wrappers or find the bell.

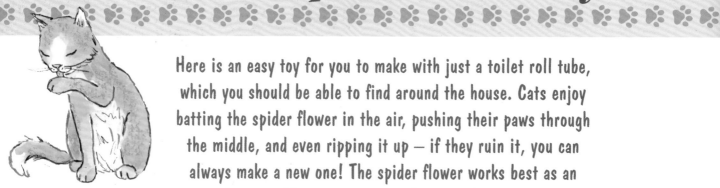

Make a spider flower toy

Here is an easy toy for you to make with just a toilet roll tube, which you should be able to find around the house. Cats enjoy batting the spider flower in the air, pushing their paws through the middle, and even ripping it up — if they ruin it, you can always make a new one! The spider flower works best as an indoor toy. If it gets wet outside, it might fall apart.

You will need

An empty toilet roll tube

Scissors

A length of yarn (wool) or string (for the variation)

1 Holding the tube carefully, cut a slit from the end toward the middle of the tube, about 1¼ in (3cm) long.

Feline fact

Did you know that kittens need playtime about ten times a day, but older cats only about three or four times daily? Pouncing and stalking brings out the inner hunter in your cat and gives her a chance to practice her natural instincts to chase prey.

2 Repeat all the way around, about ½ in (1cm) apart, until you have a frilly end.

3

Turn the tube around and do the same on the other end.

4

After you have finished cutting the slits, fold back all the frilly ends toward the middle of the tube.

Clever cats

Cats are intelligent and need lots of stimulation, so perhaps hide your cat's toys under a chair or beneath some pillows and watch him search them out.

5

Give it to your cat to play with and watch her bat it around.

Variation

You can make a small hole in the middle of the tube with a pencil and thread through a length of yarn (wool) or string. Tie a big knot to secure. Then you can attach the loose end to a door handle and dangle it to tempt kitty to play!

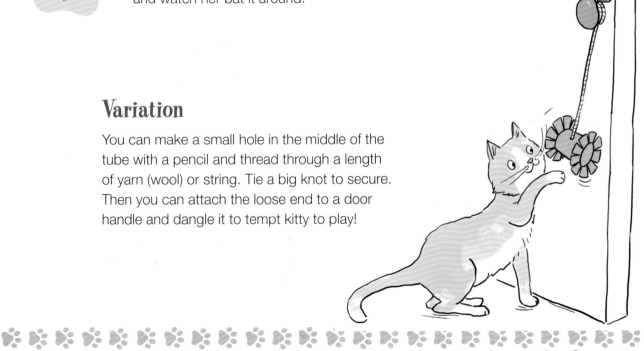

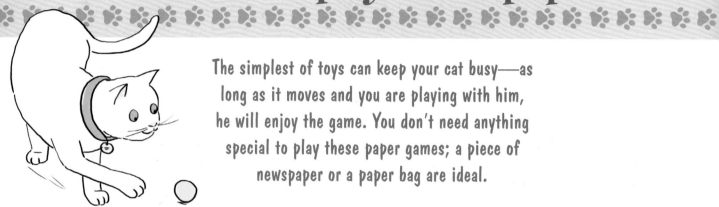

Games to play with paper

The simplest of toys can keep your cat busy—as long as it moves and you are playing with him, he will enjoy the game. You don't need anything special to play these paper games; a piece of newspaper or a paper bag are ideal.

! SAFETY FIRST

• Playing with your cat is fantastic fun and you can get quite energetic chasing around with him. However, do remember that cats can get hurt easily if you tread on them, so be sure the game doesn't get too rough.

Feline fact

Although dogs are well known for fetching balls for their owners, some cats are happy to play this game too. When your cat is playing with a paper ball, call him and see if he will bring it to you.

1 Paper ball

All you need for this game is a piece of paper or newspaper. Scrunch the paper up tightly and throw it along the floor. Your cat may pounce on it or approach it warily. If he doesn't seem too keen, perhaps add one or two pieces of dry food or treats to the middle of the ball. Flick the ball with your fingers or blow it gently to entice your pet to play with it.

2 Treat bag

Take a small paper bag (not plastic). Pop a couple of cat treats inside and loosely fold up the opening. Leave the bag close to your cat and see if his curiosity will encourage him to investigate!

3 Hide and seek

Place a couple of sheets of paper or newspaper on the floor. Hide a few shoelaces underneath. Slowly flick one of the shoelaces, sometimes keeping it under the paper, sometimes just revealing it. You could use pipe cleaners for this game too. Because your pet finds jerky movements irresistible, he will probably jump and try to catch the shoelace. Blow the edges of the paper at the same time and watch as he attacks!

4 Shopping bag

If you can find a large paper bag (not plastic), cut off any handles and lay it on its side on the floor. Many cats find this interesting enough to play with, but they will love it even more if you make little scraping noises on the outside of the bag when they are inside. They will think it is a mouse and try to catch it. In case they use their sharp claws, it is best to make the noises with a spoon or other object, rather than your hand.

5 Holey shopping bag

Once you have enjoyed the shopping bag game, you can use the same bag to have some more fun. Cut some holes in the sides of the bag, just large enough for your cat's paw. If you trail some string or ribbon through the holes, he will try to grab them.

Make a den for your cat

As cats are nimble and curious creatures, they often like to hide in small places. If you enjoy building dens, why not construct one that you and your cat can relax in together? Please remember always to ask an adult for permission to use the furniture.

How to make a table den

You will need

A table

Some chairs

A blanket

Feline fact

Most cats like to play in the late afternoon or evening because this is the time they would be out hunting in the wild. When your cat is tired of playing, let him rest!

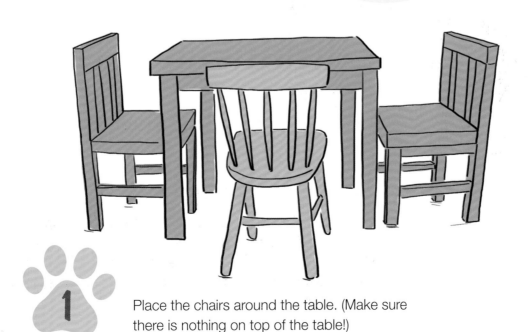

1 Place the chairs around the table. (Make sure there is nothing on top of the table!)

2 Throw a blanket over the table and chairs, draping it over the sides to cover everything. You want your den to be nice and snug.

!

SAFETY FIRST

• Never force your pet into the den or stop him from leaving if he wishes to. He may feel scared and try to scratch you.

3 Lift up a flap of the blanket and encourage your cat to explore inside. He may be more tempted if you entice him in with a cat toy.

4 When your cat is happy to relax inside, close the blanket flap and enjoy playing together in your secret den!

How to make a cushion den

You will need

....

Large sofa and chair cushions
or pillows

A blanket

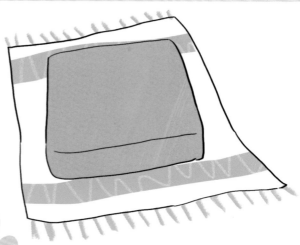

1 Lay one large cushion flat on the floor.

2 Assemble two sofa cushions upright on either side of the floor cushion to make two strong walls.

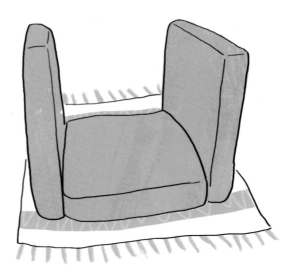

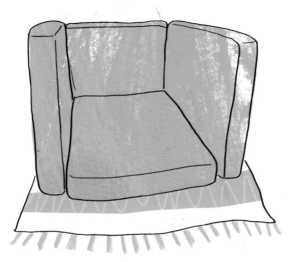

3 Add another sofa cushion at the back of the den to create the back wall.

4 Balance one or two cushions on the walls to make a roof.

5 Place the blanket over the roof, leaving a small space for the door opening.

6 Call your cat into the den, perhaps enticing him inside with some dry food or a cat treat, and enjoy hiding away together.

Find the food game

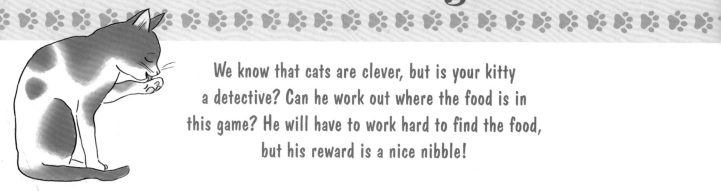

We know that cats are clever, but is your kitty a detective? Can he work out where the food is in this game? He will have to work hard to find the food, but his reward is a nice nibble!

You will need

A clean plastic drinks bottle
Dry cat food or cat treats
Scissors with pointy ends

1 Empty and rinse out a small plastic bottle with some water.

2 With the closed point of a pair of scissors, carefully prod some holes in the sides of the bottle. The holes should be larger than the pieces of cat food so that these will fall out. Ask an adult if you need help doing this.

SAFETY FIRST

• Be extremely careful when making the holes in the plastic bottle. You need to hold the bottle firmly, keeping your hand far away from the scissors. Gently poke the closed end of the scissors into the bottle and slowly wriggle them to make a hole. If you are not sure how to do this, ask an adult to help you.

Feline fact

Did you know that cats, unlike humans and dogs, cannot move their jaws from side to side? They can only move them up and down. Two large teeth at the back of the jaw, called the carnassial pair, cut meat like a pair of scissors!

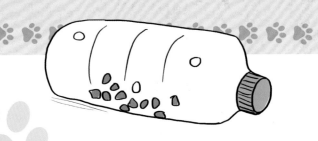

3 Add a handful of dry cat food or treats to the bottle. Screw the top on tightly.

4 Show your cat the bottle and shake it gently to reveal how the food comes out.

5 Roll the bottle toward him and play the find-the-food game! He might bat at the bottle with his paws and roll it around to release the treats so he can eat them.

Drawing your cat

Cats are extraordinarily beautiful creatures. They have wonderful faces, with big eyes and pointy ears, and can bend themselves into all sorts of different positions. If you have a moment when your cat is resting close to you, why not try to draw him? You could just have a go at drawing his face or his whole head and body.

You will need

....

A pencil

An eraser (rubber)

Plain paper

Coloring pencils, pens, or paints and a paintbrush (optional)

How to draw your cat's face

1 If you look closely at your cat's face, you will see that it is made up of different shapes. His face is a circle, his eyes are ovals, and his ears and nose are triangles. Follow these simple steps to draw your cat's face.

2 Draw a circle for your cat's face. On top of the circle, draw two triangles for the ears and add a tiny triangle for the nose.

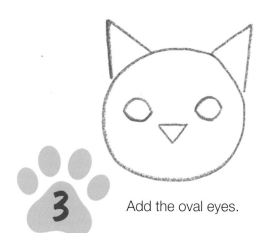

3 Add the oval eyes.

4 Draw the curved lines of the mouth.

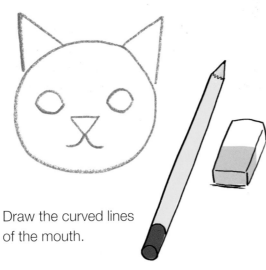

5 Add a couple of lines for the neck. Then erase (rub out) all the lines you don't need and add in some extra details, such as the pupils in the eyes and the nostrils in the nose. Well done! You have drawn your kitty's face! Now you can color in your cat picture if you wish.

How to draw your cat's head and body

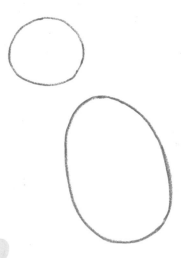

1 Again, your cat's head and body are made up of simple shapes. Draw one small circle for the head and then, lower down, a large oval for the body.

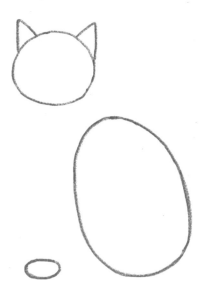

2 Add triangles for the ears and a small oval for the foot.

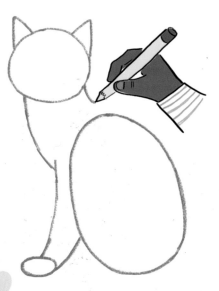

3 Draw in the connecting lines for the neck, chest, and leg.

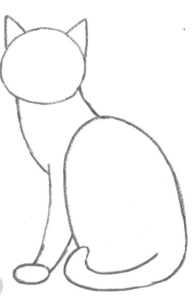

4 Now draw the curved lines for the tail.

5 Rub out any lines that you don't need. Finally, add some details such as the eyes, nose, and mouth, as well as any patterns in your cat's coat.

6 When you are happy with your drawing, color it in with some paints or coloring pencils. Then you can put it on display for everyone to admire!

Drawing tip

If you want to try drawing your cat in a different pose, find a nice photograph of him and use some tracing paper to trace over the shape. Then practice drawing it freehand. Soon, you'll be an expert cat artist!

Useful organizations

Index

US

American Animal Rescue Society (AARS)
Animal rehoming society
www.aarsociety.org

American Cat Fanciers Association
A feline educational association
www.acfacat.com

Animal Charities of America
A federation of national animal charities
www.animalcharitiesofamerica.org

ASPCA (American Society for the Prevention of Cruelty to Animals)
An animal welfare charity
www.aspca.org

My USA Pet Supplies
Pet products made in the USA
www.myusapetsupplies.com

Pet Smart
Online pet supplies store
www.petsmart.com

UK

Battersea Dogs' & Cats' Home
An educational and rehoming animal charity
www.battersea.org.uk

Blue Cross
An animal rehoming charity
www.bluecross.org.uk

Cats Protection
The UK's leading cat welfare charity
www.cats.org.uk

International Cat Care
(Previously the Feline Advisory Bureau)
A charity focused on improving the care of all cats
www.icatcare.org

PDSA (People's Dispensary for Sick Animals)
Provides free veterinary care for sick animals of people in need
www.pdsa.org.uk

Pets at Home
Pet care advice and supplies
www.petsathome.com

RSPCA (Royal Society for Prevention of Cruelty to Animals)
The oldest UK charity dedicated to animal welfare
www.rspca.org.uk

Acknowledgments

Thank you to everyone at Cico Books for helping me to write this book. Thanks to Caroline West for excellent editing, Susan Akass for fine-tuning, Barbara Zuñiga for designing, and Hannah George for the wonderful illustrations. Also thanks to Dr Kate Borer-Weir PhD, DVA, Dipl ECVAA, FHEA, MRCVS for veterinary advice. Special thanks to my lovely friend Dawn Bates for inviting me to write this book and giving me a good excuse to spend hours looking at photos of kittens!

I could not have written this book without a lifetime of loving and living with pussycats, so thanks to Titchie, Tigger, Murphy, and, most of all, Kitty, who tried out many of the toys in the final chapter. Thanks to Andy for his encouragement, as always, and most of all to our son Danny who is the best friend a cat could have.

Picture credits

Key: T = top, B = bottom,
L = left, R = right

Angela Herlihy p. 128

Getty Images/
Adrian Burke p. 90
Ambre Haller p. 2
Anthony Harvie p. 17
ArtMarie pp. 4 B, 8
Ashley Wade / EyeEm p. 21
Benjamin Torode pp. 44, 101
Brian Hodgson / EyeEm p. 11
by mira p. 125
Caialmage p. 19
Claudiad p. 12
C.O.T/a.collectionRF p. 35
Cyndi Monaghan p. 43
Daugirdas Tomas Racys p. 91 BL
Dominik Eckelt p. 60
Dr Wilfried BahnmÃ¼ller p. 38
Elizabeth Livermore p. 3 TR
GK Hart/Vikki Hart p. 93 TR
Image by Chris Winsor p. 123
ImagesbyTrista p. 13
KERRYWHO p. 42
Konrad Wothe p. 97
Lisa Noble Photography p. 95
Lorraine Barnard p. 113
Lul De Panbehchi / EyeEm p. 27
MamiGibbs p. 46
Marcel ter Bekke p. 41
Marta Nardini p. 33
Michael Weber p. 121
Nga Nguyen p. 1
ondacaracola photography p. 117
oxygen p. 50
Ozcan MALKOCER p. 99
Peeter Viisimaa p. 49
PeopleImages pp. 7, 23
Photo by Laurie Cinotto pp. 30, 91 TR, 106
Picture by Tambako the Jaguar p. 89
Purple Collar Pet Photography p. 6
sarahwolfephotography p. 4 T
Sean Savery Photography p. 47
Tatyana Aleksieva Photography p. 31 TR, 36
ullstein bild / Contributor p. 57
Vstock LLC p. 32
Westend61 pp. 3 BL, 31 BL
Wildroze pp. 9 TR, 18

Gordana Simakovic p. 105

Pete Jorgensen pp. 9 BL, 15, 25